A Promise to My Dog

I will never move and not take you with me.

I will never put you in a shelter and leave.

I will never let you go hungry.

I will never let you get hurt.

I will never desert you when you get old and blind.

When the time comes, I will be there to hold you.

Because I love you and you are my family.

- Anonymous

*Dedicated with love and gratitude
to my sister, Katherine Anne,
without whom many of my real dog adventures
would never have happened,
and who gives me courage when mine goes into hiding.*

Missy's Pillow

A Mostly Real Story
About a Very Real Dog

Author Eve Henderson

Illustrator Karen Krystal

Nova Publishing

Co-starring . . .

HOLLY,
the Mothership

HONEY,
the Goofball

HUNTER,
the Huge

Cookie,
the Boss, and . . .

. . . Madden, the
Mighty . . .
er, the Tiny

Starring . . .

Missy

When Missy was three, she came to live in a nice old house with five dogs . . .

and one lady.

There was Holly the Mothership, Cookie the Boss, Madden the Tiny, Missy herself, Honey the Goofball, Hunter the Huge, and the Lady. Life was lovely, but this little dog was very worried. You see, she didn't know what inside rules were. She didn't know how to behave in a house.

Why not? Well, her first family, who should have been teaching her inside rules, decided they just didn't want her after all. And they did a really sad thing.

They put her in a box, put the box in the car and drove, and drove and drove.

Errrrrrrrrk! The car stopped so suddenly Missy and her box slid off the seat. Whoosh! squeaked the car door. Plunk! went Missy and her box onto the ground. Vrooooom!

Missy scrambled up on baby paws and peeked over the top of the box. She was in a parking lot. The car with her family was gone! What was this new game? Her tail slowed down. She gave a scared whimper and sat down in a corner of her box. She didn't like this game. What was she supposed to do now?

She wandered around looking into car windows, searching for her family. Where had they gone? How was she supposed to find food and water? Where was a little puppy supposed to sleep?

She curled into a ball and hid her face in her paws. Her family had thrown her away, like trash. What terrible thing had she done? What mistake had she made? Surely they would forgive her and come back. That's what families did. Families were forever. She thought she better stay near the parking lot so they would see her when they returned.

Days passed. Summer slid into fall. Hot days turned to cool days, and still she waited and watched. Staying in the parking lot was too dangerous, so she dug a hole beneath a dumpster nearby and called that home.

She grew skinny and dirty. People didn't think she was cute any more and shooed her away. She stopped running up to them to beg for food or help.

Children were especially scary. They kicked her and hit her with sticks. They threw rocks that hurt, and shouted mean names.

"Beggar! Loser! Stray! Get out of here!"

Missy developed 'the look' to make scary people leave her alone. Sometimes they did. Sometimes they didn't. Many days she was too busy running from people to find food, and she would crawl into her dirt bed hungry and thirsty.

It wasn't only people. Some days, the weather was so unfriendly that she didn't leave her hole. She felt safe there most of the time. Not always, though. It was just an old hole in the dirt, but there were people who took joy in chasing her away. They didn't want the hole. They just liked teasing her. There are people like that, you know.

Missy soon learned the sadness of life for a dog without a person. She was always hungry and afraid, always too hot or too cold, and always, always, always, little Missy was lonely. When life got too hard, she rolled up into a tight ball at the back of her hole, closed her eyes, and dreamed about her family

She often lay as still as a shadow watching life move around her. She felt the loneliest in the evenings when soft, gray twilight crept into the neighborhood and shooed everyone home for the night. Doors closed up and down the street. Lights shone from the windows. Missy drifted off to sleep thinking of a kind touch or a friendly word or even just a corner of a porch to call her own. Sometimes she stood outside the houses peering up through the windows as families laughed and ate and played together. How her little heart longed to be back with her own family.

And then, one day . . .

. . . Missy had puppies!

At last she had a family of her own and the very important job of feeding her babies and keeping them safe. She did not like leaving them. Only when she was so hungry that she couldn't stand it would she crawl out of her hole and trot along the streets looking for a French fry or a piece of a sandwich. She stopped for sips of water from the gutter.

One cold morning, that all changed. She came around the corner of her dirt lot after searching for something to eat, and the sight waiting for her stopped her in her tracks. She couldn't believe her eyes! Her pups huddled together in a black metal cage, shivering in cold and confusion. They saw her!

"Arf! Mom! Ooo-wooo-wooo!"

She uttered a sharp sound of alarm and charged into the cage to save them. *Bang! Clang! Click!*

Missy's worst nightmare had come true!

She and her puppies were caught!

The scary people had her, and she didn't know what to do about it!

Strangers moved Missy and her puppies into a noisy building called a shelter. This place was full of barking dogs, confusing smells, and busy people. If only she could run away, back to the streets, where she understood the rules.

Since she couldn't run from what scared her, she used her "keep away from me" look a lot. The people who worked there respected it. They played with her puppies and kept the cage clean and the bowls full, but they left her alone. Nobody hurt her or called her names.

They just left her alone.

Missy huddled at the back of her cage. She watched with sad, confused eyes as her happy, growing family danced and barked in little puppy voices for visitors to pick them up. One by one, her babies left in the arms of smiling people called adopters. Only the last puppy looked back at her, and then he was gone. Missy was alone again.

She waited and watched, and worried. What trouble would find her next, she wondered? Hope moved out of her heart, for she knew now that she would never see her family or her puppies again. She also knew, the way dogs do, that nobody wanted her. Nobody even saw her.

She had become - - - invisible.

When a lady stopped by one morning after breakfast, Missy barely lifted her head. It was only a very little head with feathery ears, but it lay heavy on the blanket, much too heavy to lift for no reason. She didn't need more food or a clean blanket. She had no more puppies for people to take. She was sure the Lady would just look at her and then wander off to play with friendly dogs who wanted to be picked up and cuddled.

Missy was wrong. She was very, very wrong!

Squuueeeaaaak went the metal door on Missy's cage.

"Aren't you beautiful!" declared a soft, cheerful voice.

"Up, baby girl, up.

It's your turn to go HOME."

THAT is how Missy came to live in this nice old house without knowing anything at all about inside rules, and that's why she was worried that the Lady might throw her away. Dogs are dogs. Even very good dogs, like little children, need their families to teach them inside rules. Dogs aren't *born* knowing how to behave in a house. They don't misbehave because they're bad. Mostly they make mistakes because they're confused, and confused dogs just need to be taught.

The Lady, however, didn't mind Missy's funny behavior at all. She just made a special home in a roomy crate with soft blankets and let Missy have it for her very own. She felt safe there. Pretty soon, she felt safe enough to watch what was happening around her. In this way, without even knowing it, Missy started Doggie School.

Being the new kid in school was scary at first. Fortunately, everyone made her feel welcome. They politely walked past her or sat down nearby. Sometimes they sniffed the air for her smell, which is one way that dogs get to know each other. If they started to get excited, the Lady calmed them down. Nobody tried to take her crate. Nobody tried to scare her. And so Missy learned Inside Rule Number One.

1 Dogs and people who live in a house do not bully each other.

Even with no bullying, things like sudden movements, new sounds and new smells frightened her, and she was quite the jumpy little thing. The very first time she heard the music, she scurried to the back of her crate and hid. She didn't know what it was, and like all street dogs, she fled from things she didn't understand. Such funny behavior made it appear as though she didn't like the music, but this wasn't exactly true. Not knowing what something is and not liking something are two very different things.

Soon, Missy figured out that this music started every evening about the time she used to crawl into her hole for the night. Could music just mean bedtime? Hmmm. She didn't think there was anything scary about bedtime any more, not with her very own crate, a soft blanket, and a full belly.

Leashes, however, were VERY scary. What were they for? She tried to hide every time she saw one. Baths were even scarier. Her first one lasted a *looonnnngggg* time because she was filthy from head to toe. She tried with all her might to climb out of the sink and up and over the Lady's shoulder.

"Bye-bye, dirt! I do believe I'm wetter than you are, little girl!" laughed the Lady. "Let's dry you off." Missy may not have liked the bath, but the soft, fluffy towel was another matter altogether.

"Good girl, look at you. So brave! So smart! So pretty!" And so Missy learned Inside Rule Number Two.

2

Dogs and people who live in a house speak nicely to each other.

The next morning when the Lady said, "Hello, pretty missy!" she mustered up her courage and gave Rule Number Two a try. Her tail whispered a wag. She lifted her little face.

"Woof!" she replied in her nicest voice.

"Missy," the Lady exclaimed, "what a lovely voice! And what a lovely name! Whoever you were before, from now on you are Missy, my beautiful Missy!"

The little black dog gazed upward in happy surprise. She kind of liked this name. In fact, she REALLY liked it.

And so Missy learned Inside Rule Number Three.

3   **Dogs who live in a house have names of their own, good names, names that make you feel important and special.**

That night, when the evening music reached into Missy's crate, it rested softly against her cheek for a moment, as though it were saying good night to her. She had a name. She fell asleep to the new and amazing feeling that she was somebody. She had a name. Even the music knew it.

Inside Rule Number Four turned out to be a *delicious* rule! It took a little longer to learn because it was so different than how she had gotten food on the streets.

4 **Dogs who live in a house have their own bowls and eat their own food and nobody else's.**

Little Missy's fears were growing smaller, and her courage was growing larger. This made it easier to learn Inside Rule Number Five. It explained why the Lady took her outside on a leash every morning, after every meal, and always before bed time. This rule made a lot of sense to this little street dog because she DID NOT like living in a dirty home. No dog does. After all, their noses are much better smellers than ours!

Dogs who live in a house go outside to do their business.

But Missy still didn't understand why her first family had thrown her away. What had she done? What if she did something wrong again - - - like, for instance, with the pillows? Why was that important? Well, not only was this nice old house full of dogs, it was also full of pillows! Totally full! There were BIG ones, small ones, round ones, square ones, shiny ones, smooth ones, plain ones, colorful ones.

These were the first pillows Missy had ever seen, and they looked lovely. The other dogs did everything on them. They played on them, munched snacks on them, even slept on them. She thought about those pillows all the time and wanted with her whole heart to try one. But first, she wanted to understand how choosing a pillow worked.

Now Missy might not have known much about pillows, but she knew her little routine pretty well. No surprise then, that when the Lady put her back in the crate after going outside and *forgot to close the door*, her eyes grew round, and her heart drummed against her chest.

She held her breath and stared at that open door waiting for something terrible to come get her.

She waited a long time. A LONG time. It felt as though she were frozen in place. But nothing happened. At all, at all, at all!

A tiny tickle of curiosity ran through her. She crept forward, nose first. Then she stuck one little paw out the door. She held her breath and stepped out.

"Good girl, Missy! What a brave, good girl!"
Up came Missy's head. Good girl? That was almost as nice as having your own name. Hello, Rule Number Six!

 **Dogs who live in a house may leave their crate homes when invited to do so by an open door**.

This rule was pure magic. It wasn't long before Missy was feeling safe enough and brave enough to walk out into the back yard by herself and explore, not because she needed to, but just because she felt like having an adventure.

Soon she learned to come back in to get fed or for treats or just to see what everybody was up to.

Sometimes, she went out and came back in for no reason at all, other than . . .

. . . just to be sure that she could!

Naturally, with rules like these, running away didn't seem like such a good idea any more. Neither did sleeping in the crate. She thought about trying a pillow, but she was afraid of breaking a rule. Instead, she settled down on a soft, blue blanket next to a black stuffed dog named Lacey (Inside Rule Three meant even toy dogs got names). Lacey was company, and she wasn't scary even though she was bigger than Missy. She never moved or barked or growled (even toy dogs knew Inside Rule Two about nice voices).   Missy loved Inside Rule Number Seven.

Dogs who live in a house
may sleep
where they choose.

Missy had learned important inside rules thanks to patient teaching and kind understanding. She had also learned something else that was very important, so important, it was maybe even more important than the rules themselves. *Even when she made a mistake and forgot one of the rules, the Lady didn't get angry.* She seemed to understand that Missy was doing her best.

**Maybe,
just maybe,
some people didn't
throw their dogs away.
Ever.**

Cheered by this hope, Missy set her mind to figuring out the pillow rule. She stared at them. Walked around them. Concentrated as hard as she could. But she just couldn't understand which pillow belonged to whom or whose turn it was for which pillow.

So, she didn't put a paw, not one single paw, on one single pillow. Not a big one, not a small one, not a round one, not a square one. Not one pillow. Not one paw. Not even a whisker.

Of course, Missy often dreamed about these marvelous pillows. One night, her dream was so sweet and real it woke her.

She opened sleepy eyes. Warm red and gold light reached around the corner and slid up to tickle her nose and fill up her eyes.

Friendly, comfortable silence lay over her like a favorite blanket tucked up to her chin.

She touched this pillow with her nose and leaned against that one with her shoulder.

She rested her forehead on another one and tried to understand how the pillow rule worked. But all the dogs moved everywhere, any time, for no reason. Sometimes, two even got on the same pillow. It just didn't make sense.

She absolutely - absolutely! - had to get to the bottom of this pillow rule!

Now although Missy didn't know it, she had changed a lot. Inside rules made life more predictable. Behavior choices made more sense. Life wasn't so confusing any more, or so scary.

She began doing normal dog things. She found a favorite spot in the yard. She barked at a bird and chased a ball. She played on the grass and even napped in the sun next to big brother Hunter who made her feel extra safe.

And then, there came the bedtime music, floating out the door and across the yard. With her newfound courage, Missy went to find it, and find it she did! Her tail began to dance. Why, the music wasn't dangerous at all!

Missy had faced her fears and found nothing to fear!

And then, on the tail-end of that happy discovery came another,

for that's when Missy discovered . . .

. . . the most magical pillow in the whole house!

The outside of this extraordinary pillow looked like the way she felt when the Lady looked at her, pretty and hopeful and full of promise. It was the way you feel when you know you're part of a family, an important part, a valuable part that nobody would ever think about throwing away, even if you made silly mistakes every day!

Missy just couldn't help it. She climbed carefully onto that beautiful pillow. She turned around once, then twice, then one more time and sank deeply into its softness. At last, she understood.

Pillows were like family!

They could be round or square. They could be different colors. They could be big or little, in this room or that one, fuzzy or smooth, plain or colorful. But they all caught you when you needed catching, surrounded you softly when you slept, cheered you up when you felt sad, and held onto you whether you were good, bad or in between.

THEY WERE JUST ALWAYS THERE! LIKE FAMILY.
FOREVER!

Missy had at last found a home where everyone understood the most important rule of all, not just for inside dogs, but for street dogs and shelter dogs and lost dogs and abandoned dogs and hurt dogs and even happy dogs . . .

. . . and every dog ever born.

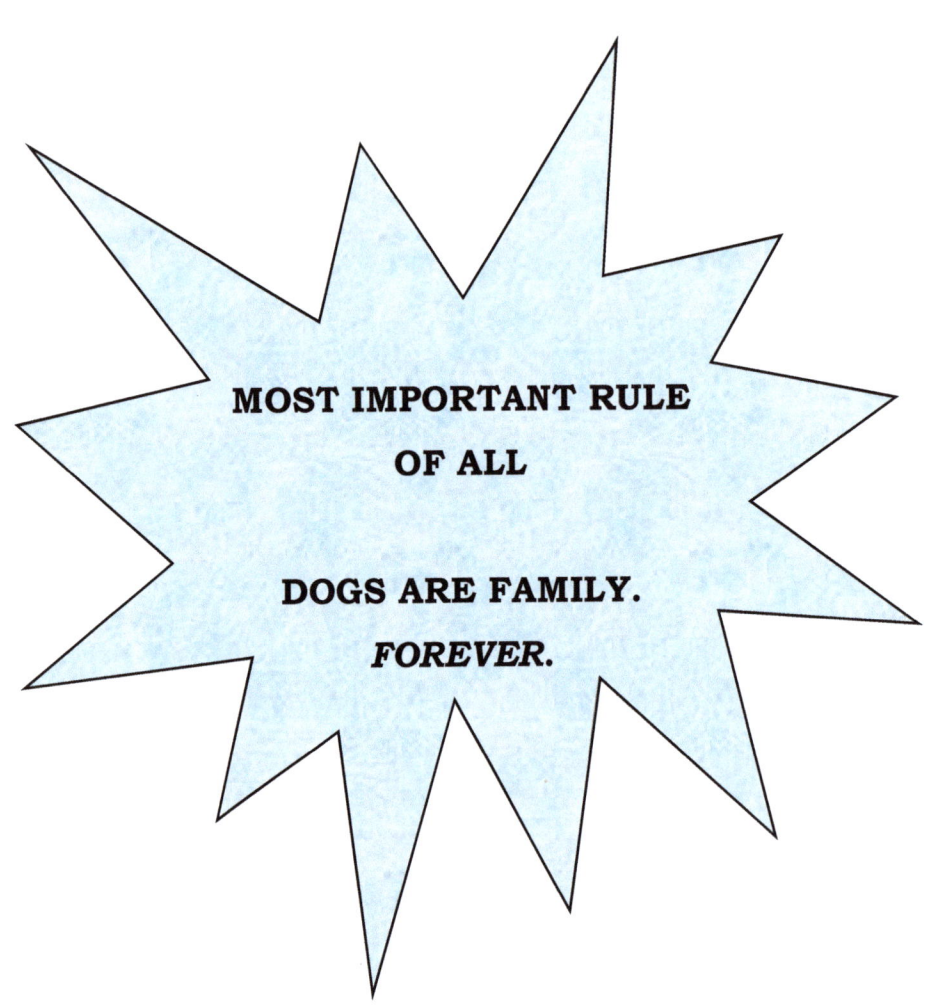

They found her there the next morning, curled up with her nose tucked beneath her paws, and they smiled. And since everybody knew the importance of Inside Rule Number Three, they gave the beautiful pillow a name of its very own.

That one was . . .

Missy's Pillow.

LOTUS BLOSSOM

There's a reason for the design of Missy's Pillow at the end of the story. A lotus flower begins life deep in muddy water. Some say the muddier the water, the more beautiful the blossom. It grows up and out of its muddiness to produce an extraordinary flower. Its beginning, which seems less than ideal, actually contributes to its lasting beauty.

Like Missy. Like many of us. We are often more beautiful for our struggles.

DRAGONFLY

Like a lotus blossom, a dragonfly is born in water. Only later does it become airborne, and so it is considered a symbol of transformation. Its beginning does not define it. With their amazing flight patterns and the startling ability to change flight direction suddenly and easily, they remind us to be flexible and adaptable in some of the more challenging moments of our lives.

Like Missy. Like many of us. Our beginnings do not define us.

https://www.reference.com/world-view/dragonfly-symbolize-1f1437926795d3cb#

How many dragonflies can you find in <u>Missy's Pillow</u>?

An unspayed female dog, her mate and all of their offspring, plus the offspring's puppies, if none are neutered or spayed add up to:

1 year - 16
2 years - 128
3 years - 512
4 years - 2,048
5 years - 12,288
6 years - 67,000

An unspayed female cat, her mate and all of their offspring, producing 2 litters per year, with 2.8 surviving kittens can total:

1 year - 12
2 years - 67
3 years - 376
4 years - 2,107
5 years - 11,801
6 years - 66,088
7 years - 370,092
8 years - 2,072,514
9 years - 11,606,077

© 2009 SpayUSA is a program of North Shore Animal League America

Meet **Missy**. This little girl really did live on the streets just like in this story. Nobody except Missy and her first family know how she ended up there. She really did have babies. Kind people really did catch her and her pups to save them. She really was scared of everything at first. Her babies really did go to good homes. Holly, Honey, Hunter, Cookie and Madden and the author really did foster her. And then they kept her. Missy really is part of the family now. Forever.

Author **Eve Henderson** enjoys life in McFarland, California with Holly, Honey, Hunter, Cookie, Madden and Missy. In addition to writing books, Eve is a passionate animal advocate, pianist, and inveterate road trip junkie, especially when her dogs can ride along. You can follow her via her Facebook page or email her at evhende@yahoo.com.

Illustrator **Karen (Maughan) Krystal** is a Portrait Artist and Piano Teacher as well as a mother of five and a delighted grandmother of four. Illustrating a children's book, while challenging, has been a dream come true. Karen can be reached either by e-mail at Karenkrystal1953@yahoo.com, or Facebook Karen Krystal's Portraits.

THANK YOU

All books, even little books like Missy's Pillow, owe thanks to those who helped to make it a real book. Missy and I want to thank:

    Karen Krystal who saw right past the captured moments in my two-dimensional photographs and painted life into furry personalities, and Lori Harris/LJ Photography for taking the photographs that lifted Karen's work off the easel and made it book-ready;

    My amazing publisher Scott Brown, for his patience, encouragement and expertise in working with a novice children's book author and only ever coming up with positive ideas and suggestions instead of throwing things at me, and his lovely wife, Hazel, for opening up her beautiful home and sharing their senior pup "Curly" during so many work visits;

    Melissa Heisey, Bonner Real Estate Management, for renting to me with six dogs Holly, Honey, Hunter, Cookie, Madden and Missy during the Montana winter and spring that I worked on Missy's Pillow;

    The Hangin Art Gallery in downtown Arlee, Montana, for graciously letting author and illustrator linger past closing time to brainstorm Missy's Pillow artwork over coffee and carrot cake. We'll be back!

    Claudia and Tony Rodarte, who first noticed Missy in her invisible moments and took the time to bring her and her puppies in off the mean streets of Bakersfield, CA;

    Isaiah Scott Phoenix for his marvelous dragonfly idea. Missy and I love it!

    My sister, Kathy, whose worth and encouragement can never be measured and to whom I've dedicated this book, and to those in my family who stood by in the wings with prayers, phone calls and text messages when I was far, far away.

Thank you all. You have chapters of your own in my life.

Missy's Pillow

Eve Henderson

All Rights Reserved.

Version 1.0 copyright © 2017, Eve Henderson

This book may not be reproduced, transmitted, or stored in whole or in part by any means, including graphic, electronic or mechanical without the express written consent of the publisher except in the case of brief quotations in critical articles and reviews.

Co-Published by

Hollybgollycreations

www.hollybgollycreations.etsy.com

and

Nova Christian Publishing and Book Store, Bakersfield, CA

http:// www.novapublishing.org

Distribution by Eve Henderson

McFarland, CA 93250

www.ingramcontent.com/pod-product-compliance
Lightning Source LLC
Chambersburg PA
CBHW040026050426
42453CB00002B/15